THE PAGEANT OF SUMMER

BY

RICHARD JEFFERIES

British Library Cataloguing-in-Publication Data
A catalogue record for this book is available from the
British Library

Contents

Richard Jefferies

John Richard Jefferies was born on 6 November, 1818, in the small town of Coate, Wiltshire, England. He is best known as a nature writer, depicting English rural life in a sympathetic and poetic manner. The son of a struggling farmer and one of four children, he had great reverence for the natural world from an early age. By the age of nine, Jefferies went shooting and fishing with his father and with a taste for adventure he fashioned his own canoe to paddle out into the local reservoir. These escapades could go too far however; at the age of sixteen, Jefferies and his cousin, James Cox, travelled to France, with the aim of walking to Russia. On discovering their French to be insufficient, they attempted to sail to America, but were forced to return as their tickets did not include the cost of food. Having settled down as a young man, Jefferies worked for several local newspapers, contributing frequent articles on local history. It was around this time that he contracted tuberculosis though, the disease that would eventually kill him. Jefferies pursued a career as a writer with relish and had his first novel *The Scarlet Shawl*, published in 1874. The same year he married Jessie Baden, the daughter of a local farmer, with whom he had two children. With his new family, Jefferies moved to the outskirts of London and established himself firmly as a great

English nature writer. His first success was *The Gamekeeper at Home* (1878), as well as a series of distinguished articles for the *Pall Mall Gazette*. During this time in London Jefferies honed his literary skills, producing his most famous works; *The Bevis Books* (1881-2) which depicted a small boy's interaction with a host of anthropomorphic characters, and his adventures in the countryside. When Jefferies was forced to move to Brighton, convalescing from a spell of illness caused by the undiagnosed tuberculosis, he wrote the extraordinary autobiography, *The Story of My Heart* (1883). An outpouring of thoughts and feelings, he described the work as 'absolutely and unflinchingly true.' Jefferies went on to publish *After London* (1885), a post-apocalyptic fictional account of an abandoned England, reverted back to nature with a few survivors leading a quasi-medieval existence. In his final years, due to declining health, Jefferies was unable to write any significant publications and consequently struggled with poverty. He was helped by the *Royal Literary Fund*, which bequeathed a grant of one hundred pounds, enabling the author to move to Goring, Sussex - a small town by the sea. Jefferies died there, of tuberculosis and fatigue, on 14 August 1887. He is buried in Broadwater and Worthing Cemetery.

THE PAGEANT OF SUMMER

I.

Green rushes, long and thick, standing up above the edge of the ditch, told the hour of the year as distinctly as the shadow on the dial the hour of the day. Green and thick and sappy to the touch, they felt like summer, soft and elastic, as if full of life, mere rushes though they were. On the fingers they left a green scent; rushes have a separate scent of green, so, too, have ferns, very different from that of grass or leaves. Rising from brown sheaths, the tall stems enlarged a little in the middle, like classical columns, and heavy with their sap and freshness, leaned against the hawthorn sprays. From the earth they had drawn its moisture, and made the ditch dry; some of the sweetness of the air had entered into their fibres, and the rushes—the common rushes—were full of beautiful summer. The white pollen of early grasses growing on the edge was dusted from them each time the hawthorn boughs were shaken by a thrush. These lower sprays came down in among the grass, and leaves and grass-blades touched. Smooth round stems of angelica, big as a gun-barrel, hollow and strong, stood on the slope of the mound, their tiers of

3

well-balanced branches rising like those of a tree. Such a sturdy growth pushed back the ranks of hedge parsley in full white flower, which blocked every avenue and winding bird's-path of the bank. But the "gix," or wild parsnip, reached already high above both, and would rear its fluted stalk, joint on joint, till it could face a man. Trees they were to the lesser birds, not even bending if perched on; but though so stout, the birds did not place their nests on or against them. Something in the odour of these umbelliferous plants, perhaps, is not quite liked; if brushed or bruised they give out a bitter greenish scent. Under their cover, well shaded and hidden, birds build, but not against or on the stems, though they will affix their nests to much less certain supports. With the grasses that overhung the edge, with the rushes in the ditch itself, and these great plants on the mound, the whole hedge was wrapped and thickened. No cunning of glance could see through it; it would have needed a ladder to help any one look over.

It was between the may and the June roses. The may bloom had fallen, and among the hawthorn boughs were the little green bunches that would feed the red-wings in autumn. High up the briars had climbed, straight and towering while there was a thorn or an ash sapling, or a yellow-green willow, to uphold them, and then curving over towards the meadow. The buds were on them, but not yet open; it was between the may and the rose.

As the wind, wandering over the sea, takes from each wave an invisible portion, and brings to those on shore the ethereal essence of ocean, so the air lingering among the wood and hedges—green waves and billows—became full of fine atoms of summer. Swept from notched hawthorn leaves, broad-topped oak-leaves, narrow ash sprays and oval willows; from vast elm cliffs and sharp-taloned brambles under; brushed from the waving grasses and stiffening corn, the dust of the sunshine was borne along and breathed. Steeped in flower and pollen to the music of bees and birds, the stream of the atmosphere became a living thing. It was life to breathe it, for the air itself was life. The strength of the earth went up through the leaves into the wind. Fed thus on the food of the Immortals, the heart opened to the width and depth of the summer—to the broad horizon afar, down to the minutest creature in the grass, up to the highest swallow. Winter shows us Matter in its dead form, like the Primary rocks, like granite and basalt—clear but cold and frozen crystal. Summer shows us Matter changing into life, sap rising from the earth through a million tubes, the alchemic power of light entering the solid oak; and see! it bursts forth in countless leaves. Living things leap in the grass, living things drift upon the air, living things are coming forth to breathe in every hawthorn bush. No longer does the immense weight of Matter—the dead, the crystallized— press ponderously on the thinking mind. The whole office of Matter is to feed life—to feed the green rushes, and the roses that are about to be; to feed the swallows above, and us that wander beneath them. So much greater is this green and common rush than all the Alps.

Fanning so swiftly, the wasp's wings are but just visible as he passes; did he pause, the light would be apparent through their texture. On the wings of the dragon-fly as he hovers an instant before he darts there is a prismatic gleam. These wing textures are even more delicate than the minute filaments on a swallow's quill, more delicate than the pollen of a flower. They are formed of matter indeed, but how exquisitely it is resolved into the means and organs of life! Though not often consciously recognized, perhaps this is the great pleasure of summer, to watch the earth, the dead particles, resolving themselves into the living case of life, to see the seed-leaf push aside the clod and become by degrees the perfumed flower. From the tiny mottled egg come the wings that by-and-by shall pass the immense sea. It is in this marvellous transformation of clods and cold matter into living things that the joy and the hope of summer reside. Every blade of grass, each leaf, each separate floret and petal, is an inscription speaking of hope. Consider the grasses and the oaks, the swallows, the sweet blue butterfly—they are one and all a sign and token showing before our eyes earth made into life. So that my hope becomes as broad as the horizon afar, reiterated by every leaf, sung on every bough, reflected in the gleam of every flower. There is so much for us yet to come, so much to be gathered, and enjoyed. Not for you or me, now, but for our race, who will ultimately use this magical secret for their happiness. Earth holds secrets enough to give them the life of the fabled Immortals. My heart is fixed firm and stable in the belief that ultimately the sunshine and the summer, the flowers and the azure sky, shall become, as it were, interwoven into man's existence. He shall take from all their beauty and enjoy their glory. Hence it is that a flower is to me so much more than stalk and petals. When I look in the glass I see that every line in my face means pessimism; but in spite of my face—that is my experience—I remain an optimist. Time with an unsteady hand has etched thin crooked lines, and, deepening the hollows, has cast the original expression into shadow. Pain and sorrow flow over us with little ceasing, as the sea-hoofs beat on the beach. Let us not look at ourselves but onwards, and take strength from the leaf and the signs of the field. He is indeed despicable who cannot look onwards to the ideal life of man. Not to do so is to deny our birthright of mind.

The long grass flowing towards the hedge has reared in a wave against it. Along the hedge it is higher and greener, and rustles into the very bushes. There is a mark only now where the footpath was; it passed close to the hedge, but its place is traceable only as a groove in the sorrel and seed-tops. Though it has quite filled the path, the grass there cannot send its tops so high; it has left a winding crease. By the hedge here stands a moss-grown willow, and its slender branches extend over the sward. Beyond it is an oak, just apart from the bushes; then the ground gently rises, and an ancient pollard ash, hollow and black inside, guards an open gateway like a low tower. The different tone of green shows that the hedge is there of nut-trees; but one great hawthorn spreads out in a semicircle, roofing the grass which is yet more verdant in the still pool (as it were) under it. Next a corner, more oaks, and a chestnut in bloom. Returning to this spot an old apple tree stands right out in the meadow like an island. There seemed just now the tiniest twinkle of movement by the rushes, but it was lost among the hedge parsley. Among the grey leaves of the willow there is another flit of motion; and visible now against the sky there is a little brown bird, not to be distinguished at the moment from the many other little brown birds that are known to be about. He got up into the willow from the hedge parsley somehow, without being seen to climb or fly. Suddenly he crosses to the tops of the hawthorn and immediately flings himself up into the air a yard or two, his wings and ruffled crest making a ragged outline; jerk, jerk, jerk, as if it were with the utmost difficulty he could keep even at that height. He scolds, and twitters, and chirps, and all at once sinks like a stone into the hedge and out of sight as a stone into a pond. It is a whitethroat; his nest is deep in the parsley and nettles. Presently he will go out to the island apple tree and back again in a minute or two; the pair of them are so fond of each other's affectionate company, they cannot remain apart.

Watching the line of the hedge, about every two minutes, either near at hand or yonder a bird darts out just at the level of the grass, hovers a second with labouring wings, and returns as swiftly to the cover. Sometimes it is a flycatcher, sometimes a greenfinch, or chaffinch, now and then a robin, in one place a shrike, perhaps another is a redstart. They are flyfishing all of them, seizing insects from the sorrel tips and grass, as the kingfisher takes a roach from the water. A blackbird slips up into the oak and a dove descends in the corner by the chestnut tree. But these are not visible together, only one at a time and with intervals. The larger part of the life of the hedge is out of sight. All the thrush-fledglings, the young blackbirds, and finches are hidden, most of them on the mound among the ivy, and parsley, and rough grasses, protected, too, by a roof of brambles. The nests that still have eggs are not, like the nests of the early days of April, easily found; they are deep down in the tangled herbage by the shore of the ditch, or far inside the thorny thickets which then looked mere bushes, and are now so broad. Landrails are running in the grass concealed as a man would be in a wood; they have nests and eggs on the ground for which you may search in vain till the mowers come.

Up in the corner a fragment of white fur and marks of scratching show where a doe has been preparing for a litter. Some well-trodden runs lead from mound to mound; they are sandy near the hedge where the particles have been carried out adhering to the rabbits' feet and fur. A crow rises lazily from the upper end of the field, and perches in the chestnut. His presence, too, was unsuspected. He is there by far too frequently. At this season the crows are always in the mowing-grass, searching about, stalking in winding tracks from furrow to furrow, picking up an egg here and a foolish fledgling that has wandered from the mound yonder. Very likely there may be a moorhen or two slipping about under cover of the long grass; thus hidden, they can leave the shelter of the flags and wander a distance from the brook. So that beneath the surface of the grass and under the screen of the leaves there are ten times more birds than are seen.

Besides the singing and calling, there is a peculiar sound which is only heard in summer. Waiting quietly to discover what birds are about, I become aware of a sound in the very air. It is not the midsummer hum which will soon be heard over the heated hay in the valley and over the cooler hills alike. It is not enough to be called a hum, and does but just tremble at the extreme edge of hearing. If the branches wave and rustle they overbear it; the buzz of a passing bee is so much louder, it overcomes all of it that is in the whole field. I cannot define it, except by calling the hours of winter to mind—they are silent; you hear a branch crack or creak as it rubs another in the wood, you hear the hoar frost crunch on the grass beneath your feet, but the air is without sound in itself. The sound of summer is everywhere—in the passing breeze, in the hedge, in the broad-branching trees, in the grass as it swings; all the myriad particles that together make the summer are in motion. The sap moves in the trees, the pollen is pushed out from grass and flower, and yet again these acres and acres of leaves and square miles of grass blades—for they would cover acres and square miles if reckoned edge to edge—are drawing their strength from the atmosphere. Exceedingly minute as these vibrations must be, their numbers perhaps may give them a volume almost reaching in the aggregate to the power of the ear. Besides the quivering leaf, the swinging grass, the fluttering bird's wing, and the thousand oval membranes which innumerable insects whirl about, a faint resonance seems to come from the very earth itself. The fervour of the sunbeams descending in a tidal flood rings on the strung harp of earth. It is this exquisite undertone, heard and yet unheard, which brings the mind into sweet accordance with the wonderful instrument of nature.

By the apple tree there is a low bank, where the grass is less tall and admits the heat direct to the ground; here there are blue flowers—bluer than the wings of my favourite butterflies—with white centres—the lovely bird's-eyes, or veronica. The violet and cowslip, bluebell and rose, are known to thousands; the veronica is overlooked. The ploughboys know it, and the wayside children, the mower and those who linger in fields, but few else. Brightly blue and surrounded by greenest grass, imbedded in and all the more blue for the shadow of the grass, these growing butterflies' wings draw to themselves the sun. From this island I look down into the depth of the grasses. Red sorrel spires— deep drinkers of reddest sun wine—stand the boldest, and in their numbers threaten the buttercups. To these in the distance they give the gipsy-gold tint—the reflection of fire on plates of the precious metal. It will show even on a ring by firelight; blood in the gold, they say. Gather the open marguerite daisies, and they seem large—so wide a disc, such fingers of rays; but in the grass their size is toned by so much green. Clover heads of honey lurk in the bunches and by the hidden footpath. Like clubs from Polynesia the tips of the grasses are varied in shape: some tend to a point—the foxtails—some are hard and cylindrical; others, avoiding the club shape, put forth the slenderest branches with fruit of seed at the ends, which tremble as the air goes by. Their stalks are ripening and becoming of the colour of hay while yet the long blades remain green.

Each kind is repeated a hundred times, the foxtails are succeeded by foxtails, the narrow blades by narrow blades, but never become monotonous; sorrel stands by sorrel, daisy flowers by daisy. This bed of veronica at the foot of the ancient apple has a whole handful of flowers, and yet they do not weary the eye. Oak follows oak and elm ranks with elm, but the woodlands are pleasant; however many times reduplicated, their beauty only increases. So, too, the summer days; the sun rises on the same grasses and green hedges, there is the same blue sky, but did we ever have enough of them? No, not in a hundred years! There seems always a depth, somewhere, unexplored, a thicket that has not been seen through, a corner full of ferns, a quaint old hollow tree, which may give us something. Bees go by me as I stand under the apple, but they pass on for the most part bound on a long journey, across to the clover fields or up to the thyme lands; only a few go down into the mowing-grass. The hive bees are the most impatient of insects; they cannot bear to entangle their wings beating against grasses or boughs. Not one will enter a hedge. They like an open and level surface, places cropped by sheep, the sward by the roadside, fields of clover, where the flower is not deep under grass.

II.

It is the patient humble-bee that goes down into the forest of the mowing-grass. If entangled, the humble-bee climbs up a sorrel stem and takes wing, without any sign of annoyance. His broad back with tawny bar buoyantly glides over the golden buttercups. He hums to himself as he goes, so happy is he. He knows no skep, no cunning work in glass receives his labour, no artificial saccharine aids him when the beams of the sun are cold, there is no step to his house that he may alight in comfort; the way is not made clear for him that he may start straight for the flowers, nor are any sown for him. He has no shelter if the storm descends suddenly; he has no dome of twisted straw well thatched and tiled to retreat to. The butcher-bird, with a beak like a crooked iron nail, drives him to the ground, and leaves him pierced with a thorn but no hail of shot revenges his tortures. The grass stiffens at nightfall (in autumn), and he must creep where he may, if possibly he may escape the frost. No one cares for the humble-bee. But down to the flowering nettle in the mossy-sided ditch, up into the tall elm, winding in and out and round the branched buttercups, along the banks of the brook, far inside the deepest wood, away he wanders and despises nothing. His nest is under the rough grasses and the mosses of the mound, a mere tunnel beneath the fibres and matted surface. The hawthorn overhangs it, the fern grows by, red mice rustle past.

It thunders, and the great oak trembles; the heavy rain drops through the treble roof of oak and hawthorn and fern. Under the arched branches the lightning plays along, swiftly to and fro, or seems to, like the swish of a whip, a yellowish-red against the green; a boom! a crackle as if a tree fell from the sky. The thick grasses are bowed, the white florets of the wild parsley are beaten down, the rain hurls itself, and suddenly a fierce blast tears the green oak leaves and whirls them out into the fields; but the humble-bee's home, under moss and matted fibres, remains uninjured. His house at the root of the king of trees, like a cave in the rock, is safe. The storm passes and the sun comes out, the air is the sweeter and the richer for the rain, like verses with a rhyme; there will be more honey in the flowers. Humble he is, but wild; always in the field, the wood; always by the banks and thickets; always wild and humming to his flowers. Therefore I like the humble-bee, being, at heart at least, for ever roaming among the woodlands and the hills and by the brooks. In such quick summer storms the lightning gives the impression of being far more dangerous than the zigzag paths traced on the autumn sky. The electric cloud seems almost level with the ground, and the livid flame to rush to and fro beneath the boughs as the little bats do in the evening.

Caught by such a cloud, I have stayed under thick

larches at the edge of plantations. They are no shelter, but conceal one perfectly. The wood pigeons come home to their nest trees; in larches they seem to have permanent nests, almost like rooks. Kestrels, too, come home to the wood. Pheasants crow, but not from fear—from defiance; in fear they scream. The boom startles them, and they instantly defy the sky. The rabbits quietly feed on out in the field between the thistles and rushes that so often grow in woodside pastures, quietly hopping to their favourite places, utterly heedless how heavy the echoes may be in the hollows of the wooded hills. Till the rain comes they take no heed whatever, but then make for shelter. Blackbirds often make a good deal of noise; but the soft turtle-doves coo gently, let the lightning be as savage as it will. Nothing has the least fear. Man alone, more senseless than a pigeon, put a god in vapour; and to this day, though the printing press has set a foot on every threshold, numbers bow the knee when they hear the roar the timid dove does not heed. So trustful are the doves, the squirrels, the birds of the branches, and the creatures of the field. Under their tuition let us rid ourselves of mental terrors, and face death itself as calmly as they do the livid lightning; so trustful and so content with their fate, resting in themselves and unappalled. If but by reason and will I could reach the godlike calm and courage of what we so thoughtlessly call the timid turtle-dove, I should lead a nearly perfect life.

The bark of the ancient apple tree under which I have been standing is shrunken like iron which has been heated and let cool round the rim of a wheel. For a hundred years the horses have rubbed against it while feeding in the aftermath. The scales of the bark are gone or smoothed down and level, so that insects have no hiding-place. There are no crevices for them, the horsehairs that were caught anywhere have been carried away by birds for their nests. The trunk is smooth and columnar, hard as iron. A hundred times the mowing-grass has grown up around it, the birds have built their nests, the butterflies fluttered by, and the acorns dropped from the oaks. It is a long, long time, counted by artificial hours or by the seasons, but it is longer still in another way. The greenfinch in the hawthorn yonder has been there since I came out, and all the time has been happily talking to his love. He has left the hawthorn indeed, but only for a minute or two, to fetch a few seeds, and comes back each time more full of song-talk than ever. He notes no slow movement of the oak's shadow on the grass; it is nothing to him and his lady dear that the sun, as seen from his nest, is crossing from one great bough of the oak to another. The dew even in the deepest and most tangled grass has long since been dried, and some of the flowers that close at noon will shortly fold their petals. The morning airs, which breathe so sweetly, come less and less frequently as the heat increases. Vanishing from the sky, the last fragments of cloud have left an untarnished azure. Many times the bees have returned to their hives, and thus the index of the day advances. It is nothing to the greenfinches; all their thoughts are in their song-talk. The sunny moment is to them all in all. So deeply are they rapt in it that they do not know whether it is a moment or a year. There is no clock for feeling, for joy, for love.

And with all their motions and stepping from bough to bough, they are not restless; they have so much time, you see. So, too, the whitethroat in the wild parsley; so, too, the thrush that just now peered out and partly fluttered his wings as he stood to look. A butterfly comes and stays on a leaf—a leaf much warmed by the sun—and shuts his wings. In a minute he opens them, shuts them again, half wheels round, and by-and-by—just when he chooses, and not before—floats away. The flowers open, and remain open for hours, to the sun. Hastelessness is the only word one can make up to describe it; there is much rest, but no haste. Each moment, as with the greenfinches, is so full of life that it seems so long and so sufficient in itself. Not only the days, but life itself lengthens in summer. I would spread abroad my arms and gather more of it to me, could I do so.

All the procession of living and growing things passes. The grass stands up taller and still taller, the sheaths open, and the stalk arises, the pollen clings till the breeze sweeps it. The bees rush past, and the resolute wasps; the humble-bees, whose weight swings them along. About the oaks and maples the brown chafers swarm, and the fern-owls at dusk, and the blackbirds and jays by day, cannot reduce their legions while they last. Yellow butterflies, and white, broad red admirals, and sweet blues; think of the kingdom of flowers which is theirs! Heavy moths burring at the edge of the copse; green, and red, and gold flies: gnats, like smoke, around the tree-tops; midges so thick over the brook, as if you could haul a netful; tiny leaping creatures in the grass; bronze beetles across the path; blue dragonflies pondering on cool leaves of water-plantain. Blue jays flitting, a magpie drooping across from elm to elm; young rooks that have escaped the hostile shot blundering up into the branches; missel thrushes leading their fledglings, already strong on the wing, from field to field. An egg here on the sward dropped by a starling; a red ladybird creeping, tortoise-like, up a green fern frond. Finches undulating through the air, shooting themselves with closed wings, and linnets happy with their young.

Golden dandelion discs—gold and orange—of a hue more beautiful, I think, than the higher and more visible buttercup. A blackbird, gleaming, so black is he, splashing in the runlet of water across the gateway. A ruddy kingfisher swiftly drawing himself, as you might draw a stroke with a pencil, over the surface of the yellow buttercups, and away above the hedge. Hart's-tongue fern, thick with green, so green as to be thick with its colour, deep in the ditch under the shady hazel boughs. White meadow-sweet lifting its tiny florets, and black-flowered sedges. You must push through the reed grass to find the sword-flags; the stout willow-herbs will not be trampled down, but resist the foot like underwood. Pink lychnis flowers behind the withy stoles, and little black moorhens swim away, as you gather it, after their mother, who has dived under the water-grass, and broken the smooth surface of the duckweed. Yellow loosestrife is rising, thick comfrey stands at the very edge; the sandpipers run where the shore is free from bushes. Back by the underwood the prickly and repellent brambles will presently present us with fruit. For the squirrels the nuts are forming, green beechmast is there—green wedges under the spray; up in the oaks the small knots, like bark rolled up in a dot, will be acorns. Purple vetches along the mounds, yellow lotus where the grass is shorter, and orchis succeeds to orchis. As I write them, so these things come—not set in gradation, but like the broadcast flowers in the mowing-grass.

Now follows the gorse, and the pink rest-harrow, and the sweet lady's bedstraw, set as it were in the midst of a little thorn-bush. The broad repetition of the yellow clover is not to be written; acre upon acre, and not one spot of green, as if all the green had been planed away, leaving only the flowers to which the bees come by the thousand from far and near. But one white campion stands in the midst of the lake of yellow. The field is scented as though a hundred hives of honey had been emptied on it. Along the mound by it the bluebells are seeding, the hedge has been cut and the ground is strewn with twigs. Among those seeding bluebells and dry twigs and mosses I think a titlark has his nest, as he stays all day there and in the oak over. The pale clear yellow of charlock, sharp and clear, promises the finches bushels of seed for their young. Under the scarlet of the poppies the larks run, and then for change of colour soar into the blue. Creamy honeysuckle on the hedge around the cornfield, buds of wild rose everywhere, but no sweet petal yet. Yonder, where the wheat can climb no higher up the slope, are the purple heath-bells, thyme and flitting stone-chats.

The lone barn shut off by acres of barley is noisy with sparrows. It is their city, and there is a nest in every crevice, almost under every tile. Sometimes the partridges run between the ricks, and when the bats come out of the roof, leverets play in the waggon-track. At even a fern-owl beats by, passing close to the eaves whence the moths issue. On the narrow waggon-track which descends along a coombe and is worn in chalk, the heat pours down by day as if an invisible lens in the atmosphere focussed the sun's rays. Strong woody knapweed endures it, so does toadflax and pale blue scabious, and wild mignonette. The very sun of Spain burns and burns and ripens the wheat on the edge of the coombe, and will only let the spring moisten a yard or two around it; but there a few rushes have sprung, and in the water itself brooklime with blue flowers grows so thickly that nothing but a bird could find space to drink. So down again from this sun of Spain to woody coverts where the wild hops are blocking every avenue, and green-flowered bryony would fain climb to the trees; where grey-flecked ivy winds spirally about the red rugged bark of pines, where burdocks fight for the footpath, and teazle-heads look over the low hedges. Brake-fern rises five feet high; in some way woodpeckers are associated with brake, and there seem more of them where it flourishes. If you count the depth and strength of its roots in the loamy sand, add the thickness of its flattened stem, and the width of its branching fronds, you may say that it comes near to be a little tree. Beneath where the ponds are bushy mare's-tails grow, and on the moist banks jointed pewterwort; some of the broad bronze leaves of water-weeds seem to try and conquer the pond and cover it so firmly that a wagtail may run on them. A white butterfly follows along the waggon-road, the pheasants slip away as quietly as the butterfly flies, but a jay screeches loudly and flutters in high rage to see us. Under an ancient garden wall among matted bines of trumpet convolvulus, there is a hedge-sparrow's nest overhung with ivy on which even now the last black berries cling.

There are minute white flowers on the top of the wall, out of reach, and lichen grows against it dried by the sun till it looks ready to crumble. By the gateway grows a thick bunch of meadow geranium, soon to flower; over the gate is the dusty highway road, quiet but dusty, dotted with the innumerable foot-marks of a flock of sheep that has passed. The sound of their bleating still comes back, and the bees driven up by their feet have hardly had time to settle again on the white clover beginning to flower on the short roadside sward. All the hawthorn leaves and briar and bramble, the honeysuckle, too, is gritty with the dust that has been scattered upon it. But see—can it be? Stretch a hand high, quick, and reach it down; the first, the sweetest, the dearest rose of June. Not yet expected, for the time is between the may and the roses, least of all here in the hot and dusty highway; but it is found—the first rose of June.

Straight go the white petals to the heart; straight the mind's glance goes back to how many other pageants of summer in old times! When perchance the sunny days were even more sunny; when the stilly oaks were full of mystery, lurking like the Druid's mistletoe in the midst of their mighty branches. A glamour in the heart came back to it again from every flower; as the sunshine was reflected from them, so the feeling in the heart returned tenfold. To the dreamy summer haze, love gave a deep enchantment, the colours were fairer, the blue more lovely in the lucid sky. Each leaf finer, and the gross earth enamelled beneath the feet. A sweet breath on the air, a soft warm hand in the touch of the sunshine, a glance in the gleam of the rippled waters, a whisper in the dance of the shadows. The ethereal haze lifted the heavy oaks and they were buoyant on the mead, the rugged bark was chastened and no longer rough, each slender flower beneath them again refined. There was a presence everywhere, though unseen, on the open hills, and not shut out under the dark pines. Dear were the June roses then because for another gathered. Yet even dearer now with so many years as it were upon the petals; all the days that have been before, all the heart-throbs, all our hopes lie in this opened bud. Let not the eyes grow dim, look not back but forward; the soul must uphold itself like the sun. Let us labour to make the heart grow larger as we become older, as the spreading oak gives more shelter. That we could but take to the soul some of the greatness and the beauty of the summer!

Still the pageant moves. The song-talk of the finches rises and sinks like the tinkle of a waterfall. The greenfinches have been by me all the while. A bullfinch pipes now and then further up the hedge where the brambles and thorns are thickest. Boldest of birds to look at, he is always in hiding. The shrill tone of a goldfinch came just now from the ash branches, but he has gone on. Every four or five minutes a chaffinch sings close by, and another fills the interval near the gateway. There are linnets somewhere, but I cannot from the old apple tree fix their exact place. Thrushes have sung and ceased; they will begin again in ten minutes. The blackbirds do not cease; the note uttered by a blackbird in the oak yonder before it can drop is taken up by a second near the top of the field, and ere it falls is caught by a third on the left-hand side. From one of the topmost boughs of an elm there fell the song of a willow warbler for a while; one of the least of birds, he often seeks the highest branches of the highest tree.

A yellowhammer has just flown from a bare branch in the gateway, where he has been perched and singing a full hour. Presently he will commence again, and as the sun declines will sing him to the horizon, and then again sing till nearly dusk. The yellowhammer is almost the longest of all the singers; he sits and sits and has no inclination to move. In the spring he sings, in the summer he sings, and he continues when the last sheaves are being carried from the wheat field. The redstart yonder has given forth a few notes, the whitethroat flings himself into the air at short intervals and chatters, the shrike calls sharp and determined, faint but shrill calls descend from the swifts in the air. These descend, but the twittering notes of the swallows do not reach so far—they are too high to-day. A cuckoo has called by the brook, and now fainter from a greater distance. That the titlarks are singing I know, but not within hearing from here; a dove, though, is audible, and a chiffchaff has twice passed. Afar beyond the oaks at the top of the field dark specks ascend from time to time, and after moving in wide circles for a while descend again to the corn. These must be larks; but their notes are not powerful enough to reach me, though they would were it not for the song in the hedges, the hum of innumerable insects, and the ceaseless "crake, crake" of landrails. There are at least two landrails in the mowing-grass; one of them just now seemed coming straight towards the apple tree, and I expected in a minute to see the grass move, when the bird turned aside and entered the tufts and wild parsley by the hedge. Thence the call has come without a moment's pause, "crake, crake," till the thick hedge seems filled with it. Tits have visited the apple tree over my head, a wren has sung in the willow, or rather on a dead branch projecting lower down than the leafy boughs, and a robin across under the elms in the opposite hedge. Elms are a favourite tree of robins—not the upper branches, but those that grow down the trunk, and are the first to have leaves in spring.

The yellowhammer is the most persistent individually, but I think the blackbirds when listened to are the masters of the fields. Before one can finish, another begins, like the summer ripples succeeding behind each other, so that the melodious sound merely changes its position. Now here, now in the corner, then across the field, again in the distant copse, where it seems about to sink, when it rises again almost at hand. Like a great human artist, the blackbird makes no effort, being fully conscious that his liquid tone cannot be matched. He utters a few delicious notes, and carelessly quits the green stage of the oak till it pleases him to sing again. Without the blackbird, in whose throat the sweetness of the green fields dwells, the days would be only partly summer. Without the violet, all the bluebells and cowslips could not make a spring, and without the blackbird, even the nightingale would be but half welcome. It is not yet noon, these songs have been ceaseless since dawn; this evening, after the yellowhammer has sung the sun down, when the moon rises and the faint stars appear, still the cuckoo will call, and the grasshopper lark, the landrail's "crake, crake" will echo from the mound, a warbler or a blackcap will utter his notes, and even at the darkest of the summer night the swallows will hardly sleep in their nests. As the morning sky grows blue, an hour before the sun, up will rise the larks, singing and audible now, the cuckoo will recommence, and the swallows will start again on their tireless journey. So that the songs of the summer birds are as ceaseless as the sound of the waterfall which plays day and night.

I cannot leave it; I must stay under the old tree in the midst of the long grass, the luxury of the leaves, and the song in the very air. I seem as if I could feel all the glowing life the sunshine gives and the south wind calls to being. The endless grass, the endless leaves, the immense strength of the oak expanding, the unalloyed joy of finch and blackbird;

from all of them I receive a little. Each gives me something of the pure joy they gather for themselves. In the blackbird's melody one note is mine; in the dance of the leaf shadows the formed maze is for me, though the motion is theirs; the flowers with a thousand faces have collected the kisses of the morning. Feeling with them, I receive some, at least, of their fulness of life. Never could I have enough; never stay long enough—whether here or whether lying on the shorter sward under the sweeping and graceful birches, or on the thyme-scented hills. Hour after hour, and still not enough. Or walking the footpath was never long enough, or my strength sufficient to endure till the mind was weary. The exceeding beauty of the earth, in her splendour of life, yields a new thought with every petal. The hours when the mind is absorbed by beauty are the only hours when we really live, so that the longer we can stay among these things so much the more is snatched from inevitable Time. Let the shadow advance upon the dial—I can watch it with equanimity while it is there to be watched. It is only when the shadow is *not* there, when the clouds of winter cover it, that the dial is terrible. The invisible shadow goes on and steals from us. But now, while I can see the shadow of the tree and watch it slowly gliding along the surface of the grass, it is mine. These are the only hours that are not wasted—these hours that absorb the soul and fill it with beauty. This is real life, and all else is illusion, or mere endurance. Does this reverie of flowers and waterfall and song form an ideal, a human ideal, in the mind? It does; much the same ideal that Phidias sculptured of man and woman filled with a godlike sense of the violet fields of Greece, beautiful beyond thought, calm as my turtle-dove before the lurid lightning of the unknown. To be beautiful and to be calm, without mental fear, is the ideal of nature. If I cannot achieve it, at least I can think it.

* * * * *